christmas stocking

christmas stocking

inspiration for the festive season

edited by sean keogh

Published in the United States in 2008
by Tangent Publications
an imprint of
Axis Publishing Limited
8c Accommodation Road
London NW11 8ED
www.axispublishing.co.uk

Creative Director: Siân Keogh
Editorial Director: Anne Yelland
Designer: Simon de Lotz
Production Manager: Jo Ryan

ISBN 978-1-904707-55-4

9 8 7 6 5 4 3 2

Printed and bound in China

about this book

A beautiful gift book with maximum appeal to people of all ages, *christmas stocking* combines a warm, witty, and endearing collection of thoughts and sayings about the holiday season, with a selection of amusing and evocative animal photographs. Whether Christmas is a time for fun and laughter, for contemplation and reflection, or simply a time for giving, you will find combinations of sayings and photographs to inspire, amuse, and strike a knowing chord in this collection.

An inspired self-purchase and wonderful gift, this is a book for people of all ages and from all walks of life.

about the author

Sean Keogh has worked in publishing for several years, on a variety of books and magazines on a wide range of subjects. From the many thousands of contributions that were sent to him by people from all around the world and all walks of life, he has chosen a collection with broad appeal to reflect the many meanings of Christmas.

Christmas is a kind,
forgiving, charitable,
pleasant time.

The Christmas heart
is a giving heart.

A hug is a great gift—
one size fits all, and it's
easy to exchange.

Christmas is hope
reborn for peace,
for understanding,
and for goodwill
to men.

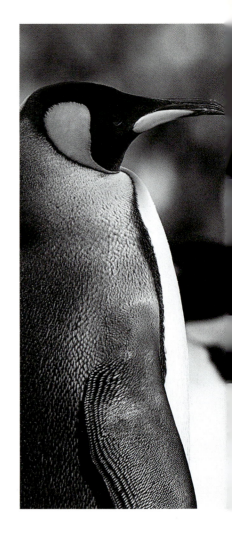

Let's be naughty
and save Santa
the trip.

If you don't have
Christmas in your
heart, you won't
find it under a tree.

The best Christmas
decoration is being
wreathed in smiles.

The trouble with office Christmas parties is looking for a new job the next day.

Three wonderful little
words at Christmas…

…no assembly required!

Christmas is a special day,
spent in a warm circle
of family.

Don't get your tinsel in a tangle.

If you don't believe, you
won't receive!

Christmas is truly Christmas when we celebrate it by giving the light of love to those who need it most.

When it comes
to giving, some
people stop
at nothing.

Never worry about the size of your Christmas tree. In the eyes of children, they are all 30 feet tall.

Christmas
memories gather
and dance
like snowflakes.

Happy, happy
Christmas, that can
win us back to the
delusions of our
childhood days.

Time and love are the
basic ingredients of a truly
merry Christmas.

Remembrance, like a
candle, burns brightest at
Christmastime.

Christmas makes
everything softer
and more beautiful.

Remember the reason
for the season.

Play and make
good cheer…

…for Christmas comes
but once a year.

Christmas is not a season,
but a state of mind.

One of the nice things about Christmas is that you can make people forget the past with a present.

Guardian angel pure
and bright…

…please lead Santa here tonight.

Today's Christmas
creates happy hours
for tomorrow.

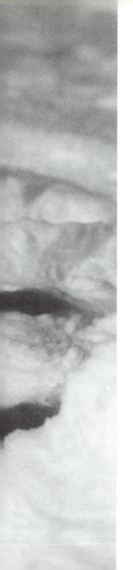

Christmas is a magic wand.

At Christmas the
world is young.

The magic of Christmas
is filling empty hearts and
lives with generous gifts.

The spirit of the
season is peace.

Christmas restores to
the old man the pleasures
of his childhood.

Giving yourself is the
greatest gift of all.

Christmas is a time
to be jolly…

…and to
remember those
who aren't.

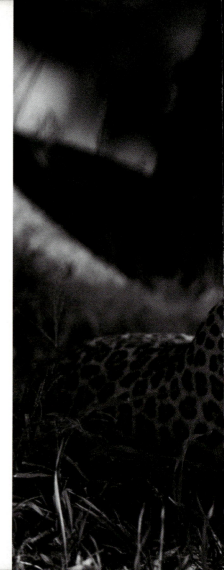

Christmas is love
and sharing.

Christmas Eve is a
night of song.

The joy of Christmas is
brightening other lives.

The great thing about
Christmas is that it's
compulsory, and we all go
through it together.

Christmas is lighting a fire in the heart…

…an inner glow.

Wouldn't dreams be coming true if we kept the Christmas spirit the whole year through?

Christmas is a wish that everyone's cup overflows.

To truly enjoy Christmas,
you must bear others'
burdens and ease
others' loads.

Love came down
at Christmas.

There is a new kind of Christmas club in operation. The new club helps you save money to pay for last year's gifts.

Christmas is
tradition time…

…traditions that recall
the precious memories
down the years.

The lights of the Christmas tree are like stars in heaven.

Christmas cookies and happy hearts, this is how the holiday starts.

You might as well
do your Christmas
hinting early.

An old-fashioned
Christmas is hard
to forget.

Christmas is tenderness for the past, courage for the present, and hope for the future.

Anyone who believes that men are the equal of women has never seen a man trying to wrap a Christmas present.

Christmas is a day of feasting
and prayer…

…and remembering everything
we have ever loved.

I bought my kids a set of batteries this Christmas with a note saying, toys not included.

Christmas is love, with all
the trimmings.

Christmas is the one time
of year when you can
count on smiling faces.

The child born on Christmas Day will have a special fortune.

Do all the good you can by all the means you can.

Christmas is when most of us are as generous as we would like always to be.

Christmas is pine trees,
tinsel, and reindeer.

What do you call people who are afraid of Santa Claus?

Claustrophobic.

Christmas makes

everything beautiful.